**A Restricted View
From Under The Hedge**

This Belongs To

....

....

....

Published in the UK by
The Hedgehog Poetry Press
Coppack House, 5
Churchill Avenue
Clevedon
BS21 6QW

www.hedgehogpress.co.uk

A CIP Catalogue record for this book is available from the
British Library.

ISSN: 2515-9313
ISBN: 978-1-9996402-4-8

Printed and bound in Great Britain by
TJ International Ltd, Padstow, Cornwall

WELCOME

It is now a year since the idea for 'Arfur' was first mooted, and
six months since the first issue appeared, so if it is perhaps still
a little early to be taking stock, I can't help but notice that I
have already forgotten what it was I expected it to be.

I think I always knew it would be eclectic – I only have to look
at the shelf above my desk to see Pam Ayres next to Rilke who
are overlooking Dylan Thomas, Yeats. Carney-Hulme and
cummings to know that I have varied tastes – so that is no
surprise, but I suppose the fact that people are reading it is.

In truth it is slowly finding its own form and since those heady
days of, well, *April,* I think it is settling down, if not into a
routine, hopefully it will never have one of those, maybe
something recognisable.

This issue is again 'something-for-everyone' rather than
'everything-for-someone' as I keep saying to people, and having
Jeremy Reed and Christopher Levenson, who in many ways
introduced me to poetry far too many years ago for any of us to
be happy with, alongside Kristin Garth, Pippa Little, Scarlett
Ward and Deb Scudder who make it worth exploring still
today, is the ultimate buzz. I could name all the poets in this
issue, of course, as it is only ever a snapshot of whatever has
happened to catch my magpie eye, but they wouldn't be in here
if I didn't love their work, so there is no need, I don't think.

Hope you like it anyway, there will be one more, at least, after
this. A year is a long time in anything these days, even poetry

MD

Poetry

Articles

The Poems

JEREMY REED

Bowie's Afterlife

Cremation smoke mixed into jet exhaust
gritty particles, ever seen a diamond
pulled from a fire as indestructible,

ash brushed off its scintillating carats
in the hard slam of mountain oxygen.
A blue diamond tinted aqueous green.

There's no backup copy, just consciousness
quantified subatomically, like thought's
the fastest way to travel to next thought

as light speed instantaneity. The glow
post–operative lives on as famous bleed
into a collectivised memory -

can't ever recreate the same again
south Brixton accent on Space Oddity
like flattening a tin can under the tongue.

He'd dispersed now into cosmic heartbeat
until dehumanised as atoms built
into the proposition of a star.

Don't come two likes of singularity
as Bowie gene - diamond-shaped molecules
glittering, repatterned like curves on rain.

Writing Outside

I meet them all, anomalous strangers,
aberrant, inquisitive, abnormal,
drawn to me like it's Chinese characters
I manipulate with ink into zen
as word partners. You've got one up on me
for writing on the street's self-exposure

a species of indulgent criminality
like keyless theft - and what I lift from you
is aspects of your personality,
the jewel-like strands, the dirty stuff that's sweet,
I do it in your face, clouds stacking up
like a sugar skull over Leicester Square

moribund cirro-stratus humped purple.
I get my friends like that, exchange numbers,
the accidental synchronicity
works to advantage, the way time slows down
in public, and seems to create delay
like thinking backwards. Sex comes into it,

you don't know what's my preference, straight or gay,
only I represent what you've suppressed
as arguable potential - poetry
we all imagine as romantic quest
and I'm the strange attractor doing it
for you with attitude you won't forget.

ANNA SAUNDERS

How to Paint a Brexit Angel

They appeared melancholic enough according to Victorian art,
a mystic sadness in their eyes,

holding their symbols out to us in taper-thin fingers
(globes containing the first sinners,
their nakedness - a blunt fact).

They seemed, even then, sickened
by those who had exiled themselves from Eden.

But how to paint them now? With furrowed brow,
the stricken look in the eyes
of a mother visiting a child
who has committed a terrible crime,

and doesn't recognise who he is
doesn't know him any more
though she once wore him under her skin.

A Ghost Before Dawn

The future cannot come without the grace of setting things aside-John Burnside

Here at owl light, is the husband,
brought back by the widow's tight grip
and backward glance.

He's luminous as a jack-o'-lantern, gauzy and glittering
as a spider web in rain.

But this filmy, limpid creature,
is too ethereal to embrace,

disorientated as a traveller
who wakes from a slumber to a strange town.

She would do best to leave him in the liminal,
glimpse him in a dust shimmer,
feel his presence as breath upon the skin.

We could learn from Orpheus
about letting go,

but instead our desires are gravity
holding the dead
fixed down to the earth.

How will morning come when the
night's scent still hangs heavy on the air
unseasonable as honeysuckle in winter?

How can we hear the one note of the dawn
when night is still whispering in our ears?

CHRISTOPHER LEVENSON

Survivalists

As light by light the great metropolis
falls silent, with subways and downtown streets
devoid of traffic, we gather our perishables,
and prepare to head for the sheltering forests of legend.

Will we remember obsolete boy scout skills,
tying knots, lighting fires? Will we be able
if needed to kill and skin the animals we loved
to see at a distance? How little of what we are
we can carry with us!

Apart from cooking utensils, knives, matches, an axe
to cut down trees that we once swore to preserve
for our grandchildren's sake, perhaps some easily
portable musical instrument, maybe a flute?

Also a digital watch, a family photo album
and Annie Dillard's autobiography
to remind us what childhood was like.
If we're lucky we'll find a dry cave
where we can store kindling and memories.

How much do we need to survive?

Trivia

I throw my two penn'orth into the Trevi fountain,
and make my wish - to meet the famous,
to know and be known by the great:
as Warhol famously said, "In the future everyone
will be famous for fifteen minutes"

But when a friend introduced me to Morgan Forster
he chatted with me about the train service to London.,
The time I met Eliot he gave me good advice
on how to avoid paying tax on the prize I had won.
With Auden much the same - small talk about Leavis ,
all hardly enough for a footnote.
 It is mostly alone we are great, in the cavernous reaches
of mind, locked in at night, with no one around to applaud.

MARK GOODWIN

A Crown in an Alley, July 2001

We are all children of the hedgehog. - Maltese Proverb

Dead-straight. Wide as my arms can

span. A longlong alley between
Birstall's sub-urban back-gardens. It channels our sandaled
footsteps. We're careful

of stingers & broken glass, briars at face-height. Our
torch-pool slowly bounces down
the alley, us

in its robust bubble. The back-
garden fences, high-slatted & private, and night's
sodium-bruised ceiling

tunnel us. Gutter us. Foxgloves

trumpet their shapes, ring visions of bells, rise
from the alley-sides as our light brings
them briefly to day-life. Dandy guards with purple ruffles. Now

in the alley a
perfectly right-angled dog-leg, a square-kink of moment:
the head's compass swirls, cardinals
rotate, our bodies pass

through a glyph-blip in the narrow straight of
this right-of-way. Then

we're bang
on track. Back on line. People
in bed or about to be in their houses either

side of our

movement through night. Suddenly our lit bubble contains pin-glints
staring at us from frothy shadows on the ground. A gentle

sniffing snout, naked. Now

a ball of darts, a garland
of black-tipped lances.
A hidden head's crown.

We crouch - see fleas like civilisation busy
on a world of spires. With flinching finger-tips I turn
the hedgehog over. I'm curious. Wish
to give our eyes a prize for trying the dark. She's

not totally enclosed. Her
expressive feet give no
thing away. Ferocious
with their vulnerability,
opposing the frightened
aggression of her
weapon-coat. Her belly

invites us to put our desires to sleep. But the alley's boundary

suspended
between
castles of
English
house-holds

moves our bubble along; leaving the hog behind
in the hedge of her night.

RAINE GEOGHEGAN

Chickens in a Pen

They drove us off the tober,
we settled in a ken.
The chavies didn't like it,
like chickens in a pen.
They drove us off the tober
you've never seen the like.
We couldn't hear the cuckoo sing
or light the yog at night.
They drove us off the tober,
the politicians had their say.
We're gypsies through and through.
Watch us rise, we'll have our day.
They drove us off the tober,
We've settled in a ken.
The chavies, they don't like it,
like chickens in a pen.

Romani words: Tober – road; Ken – house; Chavies – children; Yog – fire.

FRED D'AGUIAR

Black Lives Matter

brings me to this day on a dead end street, face to face
with a young rabbit, no bigger than a pear,

blue jays pick up with articulate claws, fly four floors and drop,
but lucky nine lives rabbit lands

thud, lies still, stunned, for seconds, as if lost,
scuttles away, only to be retrieved by yet another blue jay

until we intervene, shoo those blue jays and wrap
the pulse of fur, with two pointed dimes for ears,

in an old tee. Too young for carrots or lettuce
we know soon we must release the creature back

where we found it, but not before we chase off
lingering jays, place the shirt gingerly on dirt,

that fur ball flicked straight into abandoned lot grass,
as if a struck match flared and left an afterglow.

We wait as jays circle, then tip wings for another zone.
We retrieve that tee, its smell of game, and trundle home.

LUCÍA ORELLANA DAMACELA

Forest Words

I knew thirst before and was satiated with water from the soil. My ancestors, my former self (I am a carefully handcrafted piece, made from a single tree. I am still myself, not a fragmented Frankenstein), we used to spread our roots in search. Oh the pleasure when you felt the first tantalizing humidity in the tip of your roots, ascending through the trunk towards the branches. Ambrosia. I guess I could compare it with the satisfaction that kids feel when drinking a cold soda with a straw in a summer day. But I think it pales in comparison. My surfaces are sealed now, I am always complete; can't feel that kind of thirst anymore. But, you see, in the Black Forest nobody talked to me. I barely saw any humans; although if we saw one, particularly bringing with him a seesaw, we would have run for hide if we could. We would become so distressed that we started to shed our leaves. But nobody spoke to me, with me, on me. I didn't know any language except for my wooden body language, which I will try to explain at some point. Now, I am thirsty for words. I can't wait to hear what's next for these people who visit us at Berggasse 19 and rely on me, literally, to tell my master the words they find deep in the black forest of their minds.

Satellite

My mask collection remains in my hometown
boxed in the utility room of a building
with fish-bone antennas.

My current mask is winterized,
pale at night, pasted at daytime.

The piranhas that hunt in my bloodstream
bite with fluency of known rivers
leaving a feeling which could be fear,
but slightly more complicated and involves grit.

Keepsakes in a box, preserved with camphor balls.
Diminutive moons. Moon is also the cold mirror
to look inside my mouth at the doctor's office
when the lump in my throat becomes unbearable.

And the old building has now a satellite dish.

ALISON JONES

Grandmother Spider

Old eight legs,
your story has been with us so long,
that it's possible to imagine one of us
was an eye in the wall on that winter isle.

Six times, they say, silver threads severed,
no defeat in sight, just working, just working,
always;
under howling winds and dying fires,

spinnerets, spigots, tensile strength,
like white wool clouded from hillsides,
and drop spindled into a new thing.
You, creator of your own world,

if I should see you spinning
I will run towards you, not shrink
in fear, for I have much to learn from you,
your wheeled yarns of history.

CEINWEN E. CARIAD HAYDON

From Sudan

Hanna, dehydrated,
fingers like prunes
soaked too long,
crawls from Aegean waves.

Her braids beaded –
oiled with love
by her mother, now lost.
Mind bloated with fear,

Hanna faints, exhausted.
Sandy holidaymakers
look up from headlines

in their hot hands,
search for an alien
and see   only a child.

JOHN F. DEANE

The Parachute

We wake up in this world, mornings, and ache
because we are incomplete; there is rain, the day

will be written grey. What I garner may be negligible,
even so I will give thanks. Earth, too, aches, straining,

brings a school-house down on the children; in violent
breathing she rouses ocean to flood the shabbier streets

to ruin. One peace-filled evening I watched a fawn, vigilant
under the faint light of stars; I sensed us both together

precious. We know grief grew from the soil in the beginning
and has not yet been rooted out; the fog of our unseeing

has been lifting slowly, allowing little sunlight through. Once
I stood in a field in France, in the warm dusk, and heard

a parachute frrip-frrap open somewhere high above and knew,
gratefully, that the human heart is, at its best, indomitable.

A Boychild

for Thomas Leonard

Canal water is fugged with trash and trailing weeds,
water-striders perform Waldteufel's *Skaters' Waltz*

on the wrinkled surfaces; after the rush of it crashing down
into the lock, the water drags its way through the suburbs

like an overgrown laneway down to an abandoned farm;
small boys, all dressed in off-black, fish under the bridge,

a scattering of stiffened maggots lying at their feet; small
bream and roach, tiddlers and tittlebats, with hints of bronze,

lie stunned a while in big jam-jars before they are flung back
into their element. Baby sleeps in the new pram, while ambulance

police and firemen go screaming by. I would will him to be
non-acquiescent to a callous age, that his gentleness

may become a byword hereabouts. Peace, I pray, to surpass
all understanding, be his, and a cherishing of all the little ones.

SHEENAGH PUGH

Distant Canadian Wildlife

Moose is a dark solidity
at the lake's far edge,
a brown unexpectedly rich.

Wolf steps shyly from a stand of pines,
delicate as Agag, dreaming of deer
and the bitterness of death.

Redwing blackbird flashes
his epaulets in flight,
then folds into sobersides.

All are momentary: none
will come close or stay long
while you get your camera.

Some just cross the edge
of your eye; you will never
be sure you saw them.

You see what you see: fix it
or lose it. This is the way
things are meant to be.

ANDY BROWN

The Blue Guitarist

I know my lazy, leaden twang
Is like the reason in a storm;

And yet it brings the storm to bear.
I twang it out and leave it there.
    Wallace Stevens, 'The Man With the Blue Guitar'

The blue man with the Dobro on his lap
Is disenchanted with his sliding licks –
They refuse to climb the fluid staircase
Of their dreaming so nimbly any more
And seem to hang instead upon the frets
Like sleepwalkers hindered by each footfall.

When they *do* reach the summit, they snooze
On cushions under drapes, like runaway
Children hiding from each other in a game
To fill a rainy afternoon...as when we were kids
And climbed the narrow steps up to the loft
Where the playroom hunkered underneath the eaves

And there we watched the notes of rain describe
The glass and the late afternoon sunshine
And thought of our tomcat who disappeared
And turned-up dead in a neighbour's outhouse,
Curled inside a crate for storing apples
Like an old guitar secure within its case.

DEBJANI CHATTERJEE

Painting India

(a tribute to Sir Howard Hodgkin - 6 August 1932 - 9 March 2017)

India - you could not work, you said, without it.
Neither could I - for I am now a Yorkshire Brit.

My birthright is Indian, but Britain made me.
Howard - I greet you by name because we are friends.
Although we never met, I feel we share a dream.
It was you who said that we writers are your friends;
that we sit in the same room, you with canvas, brush
and easel, and I with paper, pen and laptop.
For fifty years you roamed within a spice-filled land,
each year a Sindbad voyage of discovery
in which to greet Indian artists and writer-friends.
For fifty years I have anchored myself in this
blessed and sceptred isle across seven seas,
where I have found friends, a future, even myself,
while I to-and-fro'd like a kabaddi player
or Rounders runner touching periodic base.
So, we are friends, for any friend of India ....

You did not like to speak of your visual art;
it is what it is. How explain a painting's heart?

Each speaks volumes, Howard, to those who will listen
to the rainbow spectrum of colours, textures, shapes;
an invitation to wonder at the vision
leaping beyond the frames to win the earth, the seas,
the stars and their heaven in India's palette.
You reached for the essence of blueness in her blues,
perfected purples, greens and saffron in her tones,
the pattered weeping of India's monsoon rain,
Delhi's royal dust and Mumbai's sweeping shoreline,
crowded Kolkata's people-power, India's
villages, coconut, palm and banana trees,
her rivers and mountains, until all became you.
Across generations, continents, life and death,
you have greeted me. Meaning is not important,
feeling is all. Your paintings have touched me, Howard,
as, in upcoming years, they will move many more.
Here lies the heritage of immortality
to which artists and writers artfully aspire.
So, Howard Hodgkin, we are friends; art and passion,
Britain and India, our arching rainbow bridge.

Notes: Kabaddi is a contact team sport that began in India and is very popular in South Asia.
Rounders is an English bat-and-ball game played between two teams.

ARUNDHATHI SUBRAMANIAM

Ninda-stuti

'Complaint/ is only possible/ while living in the suburbs/ of God' – Hafiz (translated from the Persian by Daniel Ladinsky)

We are not impressed
by your platoons of admirers,
your raging eyes,
your guest lists,
your visiting cards,
your seven-horse chariots,
your LED screens.

We aren't minor either.

If it's about choosing
between big and small,
form and vacancy,
we choose neither.

If you're playing the game,
we are too.

We come from a tribe
that knows that a versified tantrum
is also prayer.

We turn invective
into love
(salty, sometimes
sulphuric)
and love
into obscenity.

Our longing reaches for the stars.

Domesticated
    by our fury,
even the skies turn
    terrestrial.

And the rest of the time
the Earth

        – this lunatic suburb --

is plenty.

*The genre of Indian sacred literature (ninda: abuse or blame; stuti: song of praise) that considers
anger or irony a valid form of devotion.

'Dying is hard work'

The hospice worker told Jules,
and I think of her now
in a Newcastle hotel room,

looking out at the gizzard
and viscera of a construction site,
its engorged innards,
         empurpled
with intent,

here where labour room is hospice
and workshop abattoir,

here in a laboratory livid
with desire

where aliveness
is unguarded butchery,

and the lust of mortar
for definition

as old, as shameless, as the need
of pediment and girder

for swamp
         and amnesia,

reminding us,
reminding us all the time
that birthing is a hard business.

     Dying too.

HANNAH BROCKBANK

Hair

The slow drawing out of first days,
of early mornings and broken nights.
The shock of it visible: fistfuls of hair
on my pillow, or dark and trailing
between my fingers in the bath,

or tightly curled in the deepest recesses
of the shower. Hours spent unclogging
plugholes, and unreeling spun hair
from the vacuum's brushes

teased out my strength, and undid me,
as motherhood became
the new weight on my shoulders.

ABEGAIL MORLEY

Sweetheart

Of all the babies, I am this one.
The Sunday one,
the late in the day one,
the corner-shop, convenience store
bagged one, the end of the week
couldn't keep one.

I'm the weight of three bags of sugar
and you carried me that long
hot summer hidden from sunlight
in the swell of your belly –
but couldn't hide me when I was ripe.

You were fruited for months
and in some hospital bed, clinical
and white, a little red secret
dropped into the mid-wife's hands
like rain itself and my thirsty mouth
screamed when your pulse unplugged
itself from mine.

Nestling

I sleep in you. My head as heavy as your purse,
my legs the weight of keys that open
both your car and house, my arms the lipsticks
that roll around the bottom of your bag.

I clench my sinews and it's like your phone
is on vibrate and your hand is searching under
clothing for invisible signs, fingers breezing over
your belly. You're a water diviner, waving

your hands to the left, then the right, palms so soft
I want to lay my face in them, feel my weight
on your skin. Sleeping is an illusion. Life in water
happens slowly, evaporation is gentler than I thought.

Baby

My mouth spills winter. Even my veins
are thick now, ice-stiff blood hardly pumps.
Baby, I'd rock you in my arms, but they're caught
in snow drifts, hip to neck,
and I can't dip and raise them.

I wanted to dig a channel,
but didn't know how deep it had to be
and with you inside me, resting heavy
as a buried body, I can hardly shift.

This morning I'm told to do a lap
of the ward and you refuse to move.
I tell them this, but they do not waver.
It's as if the anaesthetic has already kicked in
and I'm counting snowflakes down
from ten and wondering
in what pattern you will fall.

This is our secret, *baby,* and as I say this
I know you'll never know it. I know you are thawing,
bones milky, heart valve shunting
warmth through mist. Somewhere in me
you're summersaulting in a driven wind
towards the exit, and water is rising.

I imagine your little chin begging
to be held, know there's an undercurrent,
women will buckle at the knee,
smother their babies,
or leave them like milk on a doorstep.

Baby, I want to give you more
than your frame cradled in a snow storm
in my belly on a scan,
I want to dig a hollow for your fat baby legs
to stagger through. I want to be there for you
when the thaw comes, pick daisies
next summer and plait them in your hair.

C.C. RUSSELL

Audacious/Laughing Asleep

Half tones towards home
      water.

The giggling children
who will soon
rule this world.

Sine waves
of sound:

Potency.

The primary colored
plastic bricks
we've walled
ourselves in by.

These lines
breaking
over us.

Sonar

I want to memorize
these echoes
of your body,
its clean lines
and hollows.

Coded Messages

Of pain.

Of bodies
and which breaths
matter(ed).

By which, we mean
that which means
something more
than the mean
among these sums.

By which we mean
(if we are being mean),
a sliding scale
of course, of course.

At this point, you remind me
that theory is a dog
tied to a stake
buried deep
in the front lawn.

You pick up your folders
and run,

heading for the next press
conference, your nude limbs
wrapped tightly
in flags.

Your syntax flaps
openly
in the breeze
behind
you.

SCARLETT WARD

Sensualist

Like punctuation
Breaking up the loneliness
Of the week's long clause-

Back arched; the body
Of a question mark, answered
Over and over.

Heartbeat stuttering;
stamping out its heavy morse
born from ellipsis...

A name on my mouth:
Symbols only lips can read,
And words that tongues taste.

All of it.

Every kiss you laid upon me,
Momentary;
Drying full stops on thirsty parchment.

Every brush of your hand along my thigh,
Inevitable;
The chaotic trembling of passing continents.

Every word you'd whispered to me,
Delicious;
Molten honey dripping from wax combs.

Every lily-light touch,
Crashes;
An ocean throwing itself at a welcoming cliff face.

KRISTIN GARTH

Koresh

We do not like the things you think.
We must request you do not speak.
We've made a list of our demands.
You cannot comprehend our plans.
It's better if you don't resist.
We wish you had more confidence.
Your hair offends as does your mouth,
but we can work with what is south.
Your brain is sick, but there's a cure:
we'll cut it out. We'll make you pure.
You may not feel, but you'll be felt
by hands we choose or take the belt.
You seem sedated without your speech.
We'll feed you lines. Your lips we'll teach.
Our first request: you must not speak.
We do not like the things you think.

Waiting Room Witch

A bureaucratic mystery, a hex
upon her history. Her second day
industrial faux marble tile in specks
of gleam, a witchy smile. First day display
of normalcy, conservative pinstriped
fealty. Alligator on a breast,
her uniform does not impress. Despite
a preppie patient wait, request:
return a second date. Incantations
in glittered tights, bewitching velvet boots
beneath fluorescent lights. With sage she shuns
all spirits there: apathy, beige suits
depressing hair then bumped to number one.
A white-collared spell, sage, skintight in pitch:
You cannot contain this waiting room witch

PIPPA LITTLE

Connect

Birds seek trees
that sway intricate as corals
against lemon sharp dusk
the breathing sea, always beneath everything
fills the cove as the cliffs blot to ink
just as that evening long ago in the Five Lands
we walked the narrow edge
not quite of earth or ocean
and I think: this is what connects us
even in loneliness, this
leaching away of light:
then my body remembers
how it grew life, neither male
nor female then, only an idea,
a hope: remembers the way
hopes flash and snap, can die
before their time and how
flesh of my flesh
full grown
could pass me on this path,
this moment
and be strange as new moon
to old moon – yet
somewhere in the world,
in morning time zone to my evening
he lives:
and you and I
seek that roost, return to it:
this is what connects us.

CHARLES WILKINSON

The Calls

- a pause after the pickup:
                              a second's silence;
intermix of office noise in reverberant space -
a centre on another continent? yet a voice
claims residence here & offers a remote fix
in an accent out of character for the country.
he claims employment with your provider
& from a distance adds deception to the day.
audible yet unsound, he lives in the swindle
of snow; his practice of white innocence can
show how ice implies the instability of water.
his advice is the flow of fraud, a vector for
infection. too far off to bring to account,
the story's confected: an unsweetened stealth
beyond detection.
                    the receiver's down,
uncertain in its cradle; assumed, the caller's
familiar name was designed to trick.
                                       outside,
a pavement snowfall dawn is slick with sun
& moisture merges in the lawn. The faster
art of vanishing is the power within a click.

JEN ROUSE

Hummingbird Girl Gets Married

Vows flew around her
in holy moth orbit.
Her prayer hands
held a secret and
her veil—well,
nothing much. Just
her hummingbird
head, silky as
a wedding dress, which
she was wearing,
by the way. It seemed
so white and uneventful.
Not like the circling
moths, not
like the holes
in the light. And the phantom
skirt on the floor.

Do you take this skirt
and these hands,
maybe these moths,
wholly to be
embraced in a bouquet
of pink peonies?

Do you take
this cake,
hypnotic and
towering,
humming
in bird wedding
delight?

When She Sings

She is quick to store
every sticky word to her tongue--
a repertoire so rich
one would get the sugar shakes
from it, and to be touched
by her, even once,
with her vocal chords
all a flutter in your head,
careening and crooning
that lullaby you imagine
her laying down beside you with, it
feels like being on Saturn,
swimming in candy rings,
licking your quick fingers,
brushing her cheek
to flame. That's the way
you have to love her:
with a fleeting aria,
with your entire being.

Additional Duties as Required

She wanted to be
my mother
once. Upon
the dream
of lying
in her lap,
fingers threaded through
my thick
dark mane.
I told her
all my
secrets, and
we slept
entwined, satiated.
Divine.

Is it so wrong to kneel
at the altar of the exquisite?
To believe in the (un)holy breath
she blows against my neck,
as she says my name,
fingers that same spot
on the rosary. Poisons
the apple.
And kisses it all
wide open?

Sometimes
I just wanna
tear out
her gorgeous
old heart,
hold it gently in my snow
white hands, and watch it
stop feeling.

To Have

He spent the day in bed,
covered like a sweet bean
in a handmade-bursting-with-stars
quilt. *Spots*, they said.
But he felt like animals
were playing soccer in his head
and no one was winning. They were
just kicking the shit
out of each other. And at some point,
a chicken flew from his ear.
It was a most spectacular
bird   like lace and fire merged,
so golden and handsome
or toothsome. And there was a girl
there, too, splitting her fingers
open like blood-red poppies.
She seemed to have forgotten
his face but brought him flowers
just the same. If he was hers
she needed to make sure.
Heather or clover? Her name?
The flowers? He fed her
tiny bites of chicken, and
she gasped when she realized
someone with spots, someone
who needed flowers and broth,
might slide a finger down her cheek,
might insist she eat,
might listen like she
was meant to be.

MAGGIE MACKAY

Say a Little Prayer

Praise be, praise forever and ever.
Rejoice. Sing praise, rafterwards.
Behold, her soothing of the world,
her kisses better than wine.

Divine treasure, bonnie fechter,
heart-stopper, bletherskite,
alchemist, conjurer, troubadour,
soul-grit, lion heart, pioneer pixie,
mesmeriser, voice-soar,
meteor, ocean-song, glamourie,
electric rainbow, mistle feather,
diamond cut spark-dazz,
cornflower meadow, acrobat, blackbird riff,
flame thrower, goose bump pedlar,
vinyl zephyr, voice chord trembler
locksmith, freedom fighter,
sound painter, gospel whisperer,
healer-hatter, magical clearing,
peony queen, earth queen, earth angel.

For Aretha, let the Lord be thankit.

MATT DUGGAN

The Shape of Broken

It was the hottest summer when bark peeled from the trees
Pavements - looked like they were obstructed
by the shattered debris of tortoise shells;

I walked through steep lanes several men slept in the shadows –
where the ground was cooling above a sky in the shape of broken;
Trees had shed their skin - vulnerable to the oils of earth
flesh is the shaven white oak opening arms to the worms and the rain;
How baring the core of the self may join shapes together
that are crowded and misplaced peeled away layers of skin;

Allowing the weak and fragile masks to feed
those snapping bones of the actors that came;
Spurious grins that split the bark - that peeled away from the tree.

Butterfly

A butterfly never meets its mother
hardwired to travel to the same place –
condition without thinking
a transformation of its formal self;

The circle it travels a repetition of its birth
mould the patterns - no empathy or compassion;
the easy way to ply an incidental thought.

When a caterpillar dreams of its flight
understand that an ending starts at the beginning –
the symbol of a butterfly -holds the perfect moment in time
that you'll remember briefly and then suddenly forget .

Lament

Don't replace the same armour where open wounds
are healed by breath not medicine; Take an orchid as soft as a pillow
sleep in the secret garden among fresh opiates;

Rest well my friend where the sun hacks the rainbow into quarters;
Catch the thief who unthreads such old wounds – Please do leave
those promises at the door as time will heal all of the spaces that are left
behind.

I heard you read in an armoury in Massachusetts
we shared a smoke outside along avenues of painted white wood
Picket fences and square porches; We discussed the eternal
those elements of inertia over drinks and nachos;

Rest well my friend where the sun hacks the rainbow into quarters;
leave the light to burn until the smell of gasoline no longer lingers,
wave goodbye to the road that was once broken and disjointed;
Sleep well my friend and may the guardians hold and guide you.

Poem written for American poet and friend D.G.Geis

JOAN LENNON

Agnes

taller than trees
no one will marry you
better go for God, Agnes
he's not so picky

oh
they'll
    not hear a word against you
they'll
    praise
your personality
your good skin
they'll
    never mention
your ploughshare nose
your haystack hair

but they'll not marry you
Agnes
they're little men
and you are taller than trees

NATALIE CRICK

Emily's Room

After Emily Dickinson

My bed is a cage of sleep:
pale birds; red-throated wait inside.
They bite hard, deep.
I've been lying here too long.

I sit mid-letter.
There are open mouths,
open eyes in these walls.
They don't see anything.
I would take them, like I've taken everything else,
but I am too kind.

Last night's lightning has
stunned the yard into green -
the maple has fallen to pieces:
our lost queen.
I lap up the flames as if it were milk.

An apple tree litters the ground;
yellow globes honeyed in their rotting,
bones branching into the
cloudless blue waves.
The baby screams
dressed in mourning black.

I've been lying here too long.
Some days I long to slip free of this dress,
cast out the cloth to ghosts for the rag pile.
I am the girl, the nightmare, the eye.
My own breath fills the room,

disappears into the sky like silk.
A night's wicked dreaming
lustful and long.
Moon wanes over the hill
empty and true,
the dangerous dark eclipses the blue.

Hanging Time

I live here, by the broken treehouse.
It is quiet with despair.
Stale mists inhabit this place.
I see death, deprivation.
The hours widen and expire until
I am as white as wax.

My body ghosts the spoiled windows
laced in sediment and spiders.
Long-dead children's steps
bruise the sills.
This farm you tend to nightly
bears only black memories.
Scarecrow's smile decomposes,
a sliver of blood escaping his lips.
Love exhales somewhere in his
cold walls of memory.

Twisted trees salted with snow
weep for our children.
Tears fall as the bodies
of our eldest and youngest hung from the boughs.
Their graves spread from our hearts
like black pollen
only voices, only breath
waiting for the thaw.
Here is where they left their bones.
They never sleep for long.

JENNIE E. OWEN

The Death Zone

At night I dream of climbing mountains, Matterhorn
K2, Everest. I shrug off the sleeping bag, grub

out of the tent and feel the blast punching my breath.
I do not always feel the cold, at night. I climb bare and black

fingered, over each lonely blue cravasse,
up sheer ice walls, clamber over every arête and buttress,

chimneying every crevice, hugging the face full-bodied,
against the wind. Frost makes petals of my eye lashes, breath delicate

angels that spread and freeze in mid air. They drift.
Higher and higher, I hack chips with my ice axe, my adze

a black nothing below and just the action pulling,
pushing with each cramponed foot one upon the next.

I know you follow, my odd companion, a shadow
out of sight on the ice wall. I can feel your weight tug at my rope

and I am ready to belay you, take your invisible weight
if you swing blind eyed and numb-fingered from your pinch hold.

I wonder if I fall would you look for me, search the snow for
another Green Boots, pass me on your way to summit.

IMOGEN FORSTER

Fallen

I still see us all, that day we visited
the worked-out mine: a filmy, lifeless
pool tree-shadowed in the summer heat.

I see you standing beside the oval pit,
its sides as sheer as if a toothed machine
has bitten out a core and swallowed it.

Inside the rim our faces are vaguely mirrored,
glimmering in pewter. We peer into black
water in which I know you cannot swim.

I also know that I'm afraid, and look for
ways to keep you from the magnetic edge,
as if I guess it will have a part to play.

Was that in your mind too, years before
I learned how you were found, how you
left us in the long afterlife of loss?

Operating System

Lifted in a technician's
hands slick in blue latex,
brought dripping from the jar
out of its formalin bath,
at first it seems no mystery.

I have read enough of those
gritty police procedurals
to recognise the liquid suck
as it's placed on the scale,
lying on stainless steel
like an air-drowned fish.

But I do not, perhaps,
truly believe I have one
like it, that it performs me,
a soft labyrinth of signals,
the safekeeper of my self.

So I try to think it
in different ways,
saying it's
a piece of sculpture
a cream cauliflower
a peeled walnut
a lump of coral
turned to stone
a fat worm-cast
a teaching model
for beginners.

But what I see,
stripped of its
thin integument,
is a bundle,
tightly packed,
released from
its bony hull,
a bare brain.

ANDREW GREIG

Registrar

She looked at the world
as though it had just died.
But not for good.

When we gave up on a heart
she would say
Pass the paddles Charge Stand back.
A world twitched and came back to us.

Most of course would die again
within hours or days.
Yet a few would go on to live
long and profitable lives
striding corridors of light.

*

In theatre she made everyone else
look like they were trying.

When she dropped her gloves in the bin
tried to join in the hi-jinks
her white coat stayed buttoned.
Her foot jiggled on the floor.
She sat on the edge of her chair
yearning for emergency.

In an unguarded moment she once told me
Nothing else comes close
and as always spoke truer than she knew.

ELAINE ROYLE

The girl inside.

The little girl inside this woman,
feels she needs to hide.
When she was young and showed any emotion,
she created an explosion.
People told her she was too emotive,
she felt she was crazy, in a psychosis!

Little girl there's no need to hide deep in my core,
not any more,
Your emotions show our love and needs,
hidden away deep inside me.
It's not a explosion you ever caused,
but a fear in others who are scared to show it all!
So feel free little girl inside,
I'll protect you, support you and help you rise.

I'll cherish any emotion that rises to the surface,
pick it apart until it's resolved.
Then the only emotion left behind,
will be the love we always held inside.
This love we'll share between you and me,
and finally be who we want to be!
Loving, caring, a deep feeling person.
There was nothing wrong with how we started,

PAUL WARING

Hedgehog Season

Summer, its work long done, faced
elsewhere when I saw your spiny-roof

scuttling towards our compost heap
fresh-stocked with colour-rinsed leaves

bullied down from high oaks, left in heaps
like city litter by angry autumn wind.

That night familiar grunts and squeaks —
a rooted-out worm or ambushed beetle.

As frost began to stiffen, you lay deep in torpor
metabolism switched to energy-saving.

Spring's sharp light bled garden colour again,
filled air with sparrow song and chatter.

Putting out the bins late one night
I heard your soft fur belly shuffle past

on wet grass, then disappear beneath
the shed, too busy to stop.

PENELOPE SHUTTLE

Once I had a sprig of thyme

I'm tired of days
and weeks and months,
the same blue world
going round and round

I want to get back
to the darkness of the days-before-electricity

To feel sleep
idling back to its source

Nights with no small-talk

How good to be night-struck,
to be the one and only child
in the world
first awake   and then sleeping

strange hour

of night
stars drifting from churchtown
to churchtown
books sleeping away their stories
strange hour of night never known before
going by for me alone
strange hour no one will remember for me
no one helping   no one hindering
strange hour shaped like a spoon of the Celts
or a sword they offered   *most cherished*
to flowing water
strangest of hours   like a man both alive and dead

PETER J. KING

Chapel Point, Lincolnshire

Did you know the way? The paths that wound through wiry marram grass and sea lyme's steel blue blades, then dived between dense stands of spiny buckthorn, were an unmapped maze; they turned back, crossed each other, often petered out (though always with the hint that somehow, out of human sight, they carried on). One wide and almost mundane path led over to the wooden villa rented for a summer week; the others led us to adventure. Did you know the way? Returning there today, I find that I still do.

People

1
ground between adamant
and an impossibility;
powdered, piano, moll, or an
enduring crushing, a crushing
weight of alone solitary,
standing, just, but head clenched
in pain. offending.

yes, just standing there, hands
held loosely by the sides,
not bothering to fend off eyes
seen only mirrored, seen only
scattered, and the fine
ground glass of his pain.

2
myopic, peered around
corners, dim-lit; sniffed at
bundles, dingy
slept-on sheets of polythene.
unshaven
      dishevelled
            unkempt
kept car-keys on a string
around a grey, convulsive neck.
rootless kneels in side
streets, waiting, leaving bottles,
heaving carrier-bags of
banknotes, hidden, counted,
accounted for, known.
the word "person" comes to mind,
unexpectedly.

3
savage in her kindness
to pets and imbeciles
(imbeciles and pets
are all there are, my
dear); she might have said
but she didn't move.
fell over and over
on the side of darkness,
her hands
and how her eyes gleamed,
hungry, helpful,
biting

4
in the evening, watched himself
watching the one high cloud,
watched by drivers. and passing
by, old, almost too young those eyes.
bound by legalities (a treaty's
tethering of his) not, of course,
of his alone (of his nature).
         waited a while,
patient and restless by turns of
the volume of noises,
flowing.   finally, eyes
still wide, they found him.

5
walking was a dual, clinging
thing, was a flow, was
balancing, unstable alone.
alone was
lacking depth, was lacking
one ear, one eye, was
unable to distinguish distance,
seemed very far off in
going

thunder in the ears, sealing;
there was a switch there, dangling, pinned
and unable to move its head:
his heaving static, his
temper all but annealed
now.

GEOFF HATTERSLEY

1966 and all that

That year booting a ball
against the panelled steel doors
of the post office garage

the great clanging, rippling racket
as the ball whacked against it
all the way to bedtime

Moore to Charlton to Hurst WHACK!
what a bloody goal
that one crossed the line alright

no one ever bothered you or
told you to stop
    you were never happier

Master of Ceremonies

What tripe some of them come out with.
There's one who wants to be introduced as
the finest love poet of his generation –
seems to expect me to keep a straight face -
and a fat git who aims to outdrink Bukowski,
and at one point will sing a rousing sea shanty.

When young Murphy's blotto cousin
falls off his stool, flat on his face
halfway through a solemn piece
about kissing and touching,
I laugh like mad, the whole room
laughs like mad.
The finest love poet isn't impressed –
tells me off later, the surly fucker.

Next month we have five poets for the price of four.
Thank you all for coming tonight, I hope you enjoyed it.
Thanks especially to the poets themselves.
Let's have one more round of applause.

Grumpy

The train's packed, standing room only.
Everyone's eyes are down, staring dully

into small electronic screens,
their thumbs like pale, agitated creatures –

God's second son
could fly by the window on a winged pig

and not one of them would notice,
not one.

I met someone who could still concentrate
on just one thing for more than one minute,

then I found gold
in the streets of Milnsbridge.

CHERYL PEARSON

After the Strike

You wear the route of light on your shoulders. A map of the storm
it carried in. Its clouds. Its rain. A fox will bite through its own foot

to best a trap. Light will boil a man alive to keep its Light. Out
of the hospital, you take up smoking. As though you could transfer

the heat. Your silhouette is charred against the brick. *Everything,* you tell me,
tastes of ash. Your back crackles like flames when you stretch. I want

the light you know, and so we make love twenty times a week. It has made
you
more tender. Submitting like that. Being consumed from the inside out.

DEB SCUDDER

Joan

I put my finger into the hollow
created by your collar bone jutting away
from sinking flesh.
I rub lightly, and your skin stays in the wave
that I create, a frozen ocean.
This skin is ninety years old
and drawing in from lack of water.
Your skeleton has moved to the surface,
each bone a note in the song of you.
It's a long time since anyone stroked your hair like this.
We were saving it for the final push,
which is how you know this is it.
I manage to make you smile
and derive childish glee from this.
I tell you what the weather is doing,
the rain beginning to push in.
I remind you of things you used to say, over and over,
that you no longer can. There's that smile again,
before a tear smears across your cheekbone.
I smooth it away. Such intimacies we are shy to make
with the living, here, at the end.

JULIAN TURNER

A Portrait of the Arsonist as a Young Man

As a child he burnt down summerhouses
by setting fuses in the dawn
that detonated later leaving
smoking charcoal on the lawn.

Even after he'd been demobbed
he itched for Screech-Owl Batteries,
airbombs, thunderflashes, squibs,
Jack-in-the-boxes and Banshees.

He took us to the firework shop
where we could hold a Hornet's Nest,
while he clutched armfuls of rockets
as if on an heraldic crest:

explosive devices rampant. But I
liked best his parachute flares that shed
light from a thousand feet and bathed
the whole sky's roof in lurid red.

We followed him in many ways:
flipped zinc bin-lids up twenty feet,
fired rockets low trajectory
and set up tank-traps in the street.

Next morning in the fog we'd hunt
for firework shells, rank and burned out,
we guessed were like that scorched terrain
of war he never spoke about.

I hope some part of him enjoyed
the night-flight blossoms of the flak
that bloomed beyond the cockpit glow
like orange roses on the black.

HELEN FARISH

Vision

When I read about the girls,
the impoverished girls who were sent
to gather fallen olives: that's who I saw,
but not when they were girls.
I saw the old women they became
and not even the old women they became
but the ghosts of the old women they became.
Working closely under three or four trees,
they bent to earth the colour
of an heirloom pelt. The trees asked
if I was sure, said put your hand on us,
we are true. But when I did
the trunks were like smoke rising
from the abandoned village.
Grass worn see-through by the sun
patched corners of ground,
while the sea stitched together
its bewitching blues. Unbending,
one of the old women, her girlish
deep pockets smelling of thyme
and mountain sage, looked me in the eye:
You've been too long alone, she said,
and the lifetime's work of your hands
will soon be all a blur. Then I saw
the stray cat tightly asleep in its tawny fur.

Fare, Sendai

He was wetter than a black dog
dragging itself from a deep lake.
I set aside concerns about seat covers,
my next fare. The man was in need
of human kindness. I knew not to talk
in the usual way – he was withdrawn,
but sadly, as though he'd give the world
to be on my wave-length.
Making a mental note of the address
he'd written down, I pulled away
from the town centre, the silver sun
lolling low as though it had been rolled
along the horizon and was righting itself.
It wasn't out of fear that I checked
my rear-view mirror every second.
Why wasn't his hair drying, not a single strand?

When he vanished, it didn't occur to me
to turn back. I knew the street,
knew that number seven was a shell
like numbers one to six, eight to twenty-one.
Some garden gates had survived.
I worked out where seven would have been,
opened the rear cab door with a bow.
I'd heard tell of a woman possessed
by mud-covered spirits and a howling
guard dog which gave her no peace.
Chained in the fall-out zone
and left to starve, the dog had barked
at the earthquake, the tsunami
it didn't know how to frighten off.
I looked at the sleeping sea and lay down
on the back seat – dry as a bone.

JACQUELINE SAPHRA

Whatever Happened to Carol?

She was never boring about
her *congenital curvature of the spine*
        the chances of back braces or scalpels
    doctors with their *amazing experiments*
her *limited life expectancy*
    and she was always there
on days when Jen and Meeta wouldn't let me join in

            When Carol told me how much it hurt
    and said she was going for the operation
    I noted her address in capitals
            promised I would write and visit
wished her well and waved her off

            That was the summer of Andy in the Lower Sixth
when I wore my backless dress from Etam
            but Andy snogged Diane instead of me
                even though she had a lazy eye
        and in Spin the Bottle
            Jen told Andy I fancied him
        and I was the girl
            who was friends with the hunchback
        and everyone laughed

Articles

HELEN CALCUTT

Talking to Victoria Richards

In the last issue of 'Arfur' we spoke to Helen Calcutt about her brilliant collection, *Unable Mother.* As with all of the collections I receive for review, once they are read and the review written, I pass them on to other people. It is hard enough spreading the word about poetry at the best of times and so it is good to make the review copies work.

With Helen's book, it went to Victoria Richards, who I soon realised has quite a different take on it to my own, and one I thought I would share with you.

Victoria Richards,

Reviewing Helen Calcutt's glorious collection, Unable Mother, feels a little like reading the diary of a close friend, a letter to myself, or the delicate and kaleidoscopic thoughts of the many women I've walked, talked and cried with since we were bonded by one single, cataclysmic event – birth. And this, too, is a birth. *Unable Mother* is an unfinished poem, the author tells us, whose trace threads through the whole collection.

It begins with 'Pale disturbance', a uniquely beautiful name for those first flutters, the quickening described as a "fraying of light, before a feeling of falling". I was struck by the juxtaposition of joy ("such tender forms of ubiquitous light") with darkness ("spreading, as cancer might"). It shows the unspeakable, fearful awareness that you are no longer one person, but two – that being a mother is to be a gatekeeper ("where your future and intimate dreamings are stored").

In 'God', Calcutt's second poem, the planting of a child – its care, its watering – is likened to a single yellow tulip, which is at once a happy and harmonious, yet simultaneously delicate and fragile image. The theme of yellow runs clear, here – from the "yolk of a breast" to "a golden ring". It is spring, it is the dawning of new life, it is the battle-worn scars of our elders ("I remember how I looked at my mother's knot ... I never feared a thing I couldn't have.") The narrator acknowledges that she'd never feared the unknown – until now. Until she sits "in the shadows ... with not a single path that's lit to see you". The unknown child looms large, rich with shining promise, but also fear: "It's the promise of what you are, what you will become."

The physical act of birth is savage and haunting in 'White almond' – the pain of the body "widening at the shoulders, a consistency of skins", the biting body words of "sweat" and "cunt" and "coccyx flung wide open". The final, transition phase of labour "stings" and "pulses" and I felt my heart racing along with the stanzas as I remembered the vividity of the burning ("I throw my arms to the sun"), the unalterable change ("my twenty-odd years fall away with old lungs"), the "apex", the "everywhere white". That "old way-of-doing-things heart" is scarred forever. And yet, I found myself returning again and again to the start of the poem: "We fit near perfect."

'Something' provides a tonic to the stark tale of grief and loss in 'Dissolving' ("shrinking from the womb gate ... if wombs were the musk and smell of crumbling light ... can your body make something die afresh?"). 'Something' shows us the hope spreading through the narrator like winter sands, "as if I could purify it. Maybe I can." But grief and loss return in the wonderfully-titled 'Turbulence comes in the form of birds': "There was this one we tried to save. It fell, like a broken wheel, into our garden. ... It was only when I stopped and there was blood that I realised it was a bird."

'Bird' makes for a powerful onslaught of avian imagery, the narrator talking of "the sad dying voice" of the creature, and perhaps also her own sad, dying voice – for she tells us she is contained within the structure of the poem itself, just as a foetus is contained within the womb of its mother ("We are the poem").

"Death," we see in 'Melon Picker', "touched your feet with its wing". There is rage, here: from "the pain of broken feet", where the unnamed 'you' "knelt under the night's drunken expanse, bleeding the lines". The sun, here, in contrast to the earlier tone of 'God', is "bloat gold, over black boulder seeds, knocking like enormous breasts". The narrator talks of a "toll" – the toll of maternal love, that carries us back, time and again, to our experience of the "barren harvest".

There is the mourning of romantic love here, too. In 'North Light', the narrator talks of love "like a pale sheet, sunk against the pale earth". I imagine a couple separated by some "marbled absence", their once-dancing mouths "lustreless", "empty-lapped"; space between them marked by a "pale sky". And in the same, rich vein, the voice in 'Teeth' is angry. The narrator asks her partner to "make a woman instead of some lying leaf. Or totem of grief." She wants to be understood, without having to say the words. She wants to be left alone to grieve. And in 'The Gardener' we hear of "this mode of a man I've learned to love", a man who "wants it all to burn". As a couple, they have committed themselves "to this blood-red insistence".

The imagery is rich and complex throughout, filled with its own totems: birds crash-land, lotus flowers bloom in the shadows, grief burns bright and painful as the sun. Boats rock, unsteady. Horses are either stabled or walk on "like women through fire". Blood pools, sticky and cloying. Death is life, life is birth, and birth is also death. Calcutt's poems reduce us to our animal essence. Some lines linger with me, long after the rest. This, from Crossing: "And by field, I mean the resting place of my daughter. The animal world that keeps her, before I wake her." And from the title poem, aptly, 'Unable Mother': "It's like squeezing flesh and fruit from the bone, this terrible love." This savage, frightening, atavistic love. Motherhood.

Unable Mother is available from V Press, at: vpresspoetry.blogspot.com

DAVID MARK WILLIAMS

What Am I Reading?

Because his name has popped up quite a lot in the pages of
Arfur, I have been prompted to renew my acquaintance with
Brian Patten, a poet hero of mine since I was a teenager. I've
been reading *Little Johnny's Confession*, his debut collection,
first published in 1967, most of which he wrote between the
ages of 18 and 19 (although some were written when he was even
younger), a fact that appealed to me at the time. It's a remarkable
achievement. The maturity of the voice is impressive. I especially love
the Little Johnny poems, having a penchant for poem series featuring
an eponymous character. The Robinson poems of Weldon Kees are
another favourite. Patten's progression is often regarded as becoming
more refined after his first book but I do relish the pure raw talent of
his first offering. On the other hand, and not to oversimplify, the book
does also contain several of his most exquisite lyrics, poems that stand
up well regardless of when they were written, like In a New Kind of
Dawn with its haunting final couplet "& lives you'd have swum
through/had you been strong enough", which certainly resonated for
me at the time and still does. I must have read these early poems many
times over because on re-reading they are very familiar, like meeting up
with old friends, but there's the pleasure of being reminded of their
energy and inventiveness. It was reassuring to discover that the poems
in Little Johnny's Confession haven't palled for me one little bit, they
are still as fresh and vibrant as ever.

LUKE HAINES

Smashing The System

Genius, it is such a funny word. Used every day to describe somebody who can kick a ball, take a tune, slow it down and sell it to John Lewis for their Christmas advert, or even create a new theory in the realm of cold fusion.

Genius. To use it is almost counter-productive, by giving somebody that 'accolade' you are almost saying the opposite. Which is worrying, as I probably say it far too often. That and 'brilliant', with the same issues.

However, some people, within their realm are genuinely and completely at odds, see the world in a different way from the rest of us and when they set their madly, fevered, brilliant minds in the direction of their art, well they may not be a genius as such, but the results can sometimes be and that is something quite different.

I need to think about that a little more.

Getting to the point, I try each time Arfur is published to have included a songwriter and this time I am lucky enough to have spoken to Luke Haines, once of a band called The Auteurs, another called Baader Meinhoff and then there was Black Box Recorder for good measure.

He is a chap who goes his own way, a path that is genuinely one untrod. Like many artists, he has only enjoyed fleeting fame, but has created art that at times is utterly compelling, at others, like no other. He probably wouldn't agree, but his album *Smashing The System* was his *Sgt. Pepper's*, *Pet Sounds* or *Velvet Underground & Nico*, perhaps even his *Victorialand*. Whatever, it is many kinds of brilliant and unlike anything else you will have heard. I was happy to talk to Luke about the album, here is how it went.

The Auteurs and 'Model' led to a Mercury Award nomination and is probably the time that most people will have heard of you from. Do you get fed-up of people asking him about music you made over 20 years ago?

"No, I really don't care, it is nice in a way as I have made lots of records and if they still matter to people it is great and it is only fair to talk about them"

Obviously, the Auteurs was the first band where you had control, but before that you appeared in The Servants. How did your experience in The Servants shape how you wanted to do things with the Auteurs?

"With The Servants I was just there to be a guitar player and nothing more. They already were writing really strong songs, so it was a great opportunity to learn how to write songs, and then all the recording side of things too. I think you develop an instinct about what works and what doesn't and I had the chance to gain that before it was all on my shoulders".

When the Auteurs debut album "New Wave" came out, I remember feeling that for a debut it was very precise compared to what a lot of other first albums were like,

"In a way it felt like my second album as I suppose I'd made all my mistakes or seen them with The Servants, so I was a little ahead of some of the other bands."

Moving forward, you recorded at one point as the 'Baeder Meinhoff', and 1960/1970s European Terrorism is a recurring theme in your work. What attracts you to it? Is it as simple as modern terrorism is rubbish?

"I really don't know what it is, I think it is just growing up at that time it stayed with me, it gets into your head. I guess I like experimentation so in my mind I saw terrorism mixing up with some really hardcore Funk - so yes, a mixture of terror and funk. (laughing)"

When you came to record "Smash The System", it was your first album of songs after a number of concept albums. To say this is like nothing else, is really to undersell it, can you tell us how the songs came to be written?

"I spent a lot of time trying out new/old synths, discovering new sounds. I'm a big believer in analogue gear, the synths especially just seem to have their own sound rather than trying to be something they aren't, like with digital. As for the songs, they are all about the times we live in and whilst I can't really - the song isn't the place to - give empathy or guidance, I chose to go surreal with it and discover pathways like that."

The first song on the album is "Ulrike Meinhof's Brain Is Missing", tell us about that,

"It is a real story, a crazy and crazed tale of his daughter's quest to find his brain which quite literally did go missing. This is hallucinogenic in its scope, but like the rest of the album there is a serious attempt to write a song that matches he times, the craziness of the times. I think strong song-writing has to underpin everything else that is happening, which is important as the words are really important but they can't swamp the fact that it is meant to be a song."

What is your approach to recording, the album feels as though you have taken forever to work on every detail?

"I have my own studio thankfully, and have used it for the last six albums. The type of music I make would be impossible in commercial studios as the costs would be prohibitively expensive as you are right, I can spend large amounts of time on really small details. I am not a perfectionist looking for the impossible, I just have my own method. It works for me."

The second song on the album is "Black Bunny (I'm Not Vince Taylor)" how would you describe that?

"Black Bunny is a 'What-if' of a song, dedicated as much to Ziggy Stardust as Vince Taylor. It opens with a riot of fuzz wah guitar before it descends into a Theme-from-Pong soundtrack. This was a nightmare and took forever to mix."

Can you tell us a little about a few of the other songs?

"I won't go through every song, but the Bomber Jacket, is a song dating back to the Auteurs and is a very simple collection of imagery that anybody that grew-up in the 1970s would recognise. This took years to unveil itself to me, and I'm not even sure now that it will ever really be finished. Another that is like that was "Bruce Lee, Roman Polanski and

Me" which explores the (allegedly) true story of the film-maker Roman Polanski who was convinced that Bruce Lee was responsible for the death of Sharon Tate, even after Charles Manson was convicted. The filmmaker even hired private detectives to try and prove Lee's guilt. Another is 'Cosmic Man' which in many ways is a personal manifesto. The song, "Smash The System" took a long time to feel right as it is a genuine cry. I always feel that there are songs that you would record when you are 18 that perhaps you would think too much about later and this is an example of that, so I deliberately just went for it. This is a song above politics, where listening to Davey Jones of the Monkees makes you realise that he, and music generally, is a higher force for good than any political leader that ever li(v)ed. And the album ends with a quite fitting "Are You Mad?", with is a perfect comedown, a down to earth song that obsesses over the simple fact that we are born fucking mad and we die fucking mad. It is the one fact of life, the way of humankind."

Which just about sums it up.

Luke Haines 'Smash The System' came out a few years ago, but genius doesn't fade however little light it sometimes receives.

KRISTIN GARTH & TIANNA HANSEN

Talking to Amy Alexander

We live in quite confusing times and in many ways it is frightening that politically and socially, ideas and ideals we thought long dead and discredited are seemingly infecting the mainstream again. Somehow it has become acceptable to be able to lie outrageously, to hate people for their sex, race, weight, disabilities or life choices and then just claim any criticism is 'fake news.'

You would have to be living under a very well-hidden rock not to have noticed the Kavanaugh nomination 'process' in recent times, and a year after the #metoo campaign began, from the UK, even by the lowly standards of some of our own politicians, it still seems amazing that such a position can be filled without taking the time to at least investigate such accusations. But what can you do?

Well, I am pleased to say that Amy Alexander took the opportunity to talk to two poets, who are trying to do *something*; Kristin Garth and Tianna Hansen, of Rhythm & Bones are pouring their experiences and energy into an anthology of poetry that aims to give women a voice, that so many in the media and the political world seem intent on ignoring.. I'm proud to share their conversation here.

Amy Alexander,

On July 9, 2018, U.S. President Donald Trump nominated Brett Kavanaugh to become a justice in the Supreme Court. Over the course of the next two months, Dr. Christine Blasey Ford came forth alleging that she was sexually assaulted by Kavanaugh while she was in high school. On September 27, Kavanaugh and Ford testified before the

Senate Judiciary Committee about what happened all those years ago. Many who watched or listened to the hearings felt triggered by both the raw memories presented by Ford and also the callous attitude of Kavanaugh and many on the committee--and in the country--toward Ford. In response to the news of Ford coming forward to speak about her experiences, poet Kristin Garth felt compelled to post on Twitter her support of Ford, and encouraged other sexual assault survivors to post their writings as a way of supporting of Ford and in protest of Kavanaugh. The thread stretched on for days.

At this, poet and editor Tianna Hansen, of Rhythm & Bones Literary Magazine and Press, decided to create an anthology of writings about sexual assault and its aftermath, and asked Garth to co-edit the anthology, titled *You Are Not Your Rape*. The anthology has raised $685, to date, on Kickstarter, with a large portion of those funds going to support rape crisis organizations.

I spoke with Hansen and Garth about their project the day after the testimonies took place.

Alexander: It seems fitting that we would chat today, after yesterday's testimonies. When you posted that thread, did you anticipate that it might become something bigger?

Garth: No, but I guess you always hope. The poetry community on Twitter is so active and supportive that perhaps someone would see a need for these voices to be heard. It happened very quickly though. Tianna is so wonderful, and I knew when she, in particular, said that she wanted to do this, it would go down fast and powerful because she is a Capricorn. I know how she operates. I trust her absolutely!

Alexander: Tianna, what goes through your body and heart and mind when you see a project that you know is something you have to take on?

Hansen: When I see a project such as the one that Kristin invigorated in me through her post regarding bringing together people who have survived and experienced sexual assault, which is a topic that is very dear to me, I become enchanted with it, it won't leave my mind, like I have been struck by lightning, almost. I had a line from one of my creative nonfiction pieces regarding my own sexual abuse and assault that wouldn't leave my head after I saw Kristin's post: "You are not your rape." And I got the idea of giving all these stunning voices a permanent home. It felt like an appropriate title for such an influential and important project and my entire heart began to glow with it. That may sound corny, but that's how it kinda happens for me. Such an intense yearning to make it happen, so I just did it and offered Kristin to partner with me and was so pleased she agreed!

Alexander: Thank you for describing the physical sensation that comes along with pursuing meaningful work. I think that is an aspect of creating and commerce that goes unspoken, but is very important.

Hansen: I agree. That's the best way I know I have to create something, when I become physically enamored with an idea, the same way I started Rhythm & Bones, I just know it can't go wrong. I know it would be harder to not do it than to do it, if that makes sense (chuckles).

Alexander: Did you listen to the Kavanaugh hearings yesterday? Whether or not you did, it was difficult not to be aware of the impact that was having on the survivor community. How did you cope with it all?

Hansen: I could only bring myself to listen to Dr. Ford's testimony, fully. She was so brave, I could see she struggled to get through the recollection and I cannot imagine taking on something like that. I saw some of the hearing when I got home, and one senator was saying how Kavanaugh is just as much of a victim, which tore me to pieces inside, I couldn't bear to watch anymore. I tried to reach out to the survivor community and let them know they are not alone. I think Rhythm & Bones is such a great place for those dealing with trauma to come together, and that was my entire purpose for creating that. Especially now, with this anthology, I hope we can really make an impact. It means so much to me to allow survivors to know they are not alone and they are so brave, they are heard no matter what. Even if the rest of the world isn't listening, we hear them. We feel them. We see them and believe them.

Garth: I managed to watch the entire hearing. It crushed me. Christine Blasey Ford was an honest, credible witness. It was so hard to watch her suffering compared to the tantrum of a man who was offended he had to account for his past in the biggest job interview in our country in the legal profession. I haven't watched coverage today because it is too much. I am very sad today.

Alexander. Tell me, without giving too much away, about some of the ooh and ahh and aha moments you have had reading these submissions.

Garth. The artistry of these poems, it really is a testament that you can make a thing of great beauty out of an absolute tragedy. There is a poem that jumps to mind that had the most amazing circus and clown imagery. It was so inventive in how it dealt with this person's feeling about what happened to their underage body.

Hansen. This morning we got one that began with the line, "How do you fake a death that's already happened?" That really stunned both of us I think.

Alexander. Do you recall the first time you wrote about your assaults, and what that was like for you?

Hansen. The first time I brought myself to write about anything like that was (instead of my assault), an emotionally and physically abusive relationship I suffered in, which turned into a CNF piece "Never Love Me That Way." In writing that, I started to discover I was also sexually abused in that relationship too but had kind of stamped it down, ignoring it. I didn't really realize the extent of my previous ex's abuse on me until I started speaking to others who told me "that's not ok". Writing felt like the best way to get it out and it became a cathartic release, so that for a long time, and even now, it's nearly all I can write about. My husband became very concerned, asking me why I was going so deep and so dark. He thought it was making it worse, but I explained to him, it makes me better. I need to get it out, to talk and write about it and share it. I'm not ashamed anymore about what happened. It's real, it happened, and I hope my stories will help others. The first time I wrote about the actual assaults, though, were in poetry form. I couldn't bear to write creative nonfiction about it, almost like in poetry, it was easier to let it flow. I just had a poem accepted, "Clean Shaven," that is probably the most I have revealed about my constant assaults in that abusive relationship and writing that was difficult but so relieving and worthwhile. I think that will find its way into the anthology. I still find it hard, though. Even now, I'm shaking a little talking about it. So even though I find it necessary and cathartic, it also can be such a struggle.

Garth: I have always written about my abuse and my sexuality in my poetry. I think a lot of my sexuality has been formed by my abuse history, and I very much think the personal is political. It's why I think it's very relevant that a Supreme Court justice who seeks to subjugate women, take away reproductive rights who is also an alleged rapist, that's very relevant. It shows that it is his character to deny women of their rights. I write a lot about power imbalances and men, Puritans specifically, who abuse their power in regards to women. To me, it has been a theme of my life, and I recognize that pain when I see it in other places in the world. It speaks to me, and I feel like I do a decent job making that case.

Alexander: What advice do you have for your fellow survivors when it comes to expressing yourself, supporting others, and also taking a break to process and heal?

Garth: You have to take breaks. Last night, I just had to tell people on Twitter, I am not okay. Please be patient with me right now.

Hansen: Don't be afraid. It can be a daunting, intimidating task, but also be aware of yourself and how you are feeling. If you aren't ready to express it, don't feel like you have to just because others are at the point where that is what they are doing. Like Kristin said the other day and I think this is so true, Empowerment is a process. It takes all stages to get there, many of them very dark. Also reaching out to those you can see are struggling is so important and offering them support. A caring, loving community can do so much in the ways of healing and overcoming these horrible things we have all endured.

You can find out more at www.facebook.com/rhythmboneslit

GENYA JOHNSON

What Am I Reading?

P oems of the Underground is a collection of poetry by a wide range of authors. The idea behind the book came from a group of people who began filling up empty advertising spaces with poetry, on the underground. (With permission of course) This became hugely successful and people began to enjoy reading poetry as they travelled, instead of the usual advertisements. Both the Arts Council and Faber and Faber came on board to sponsor the idea.

Poems On The Underground was officially launched at Aldwych station on the 29th January 1986. Poems were scattered around the stations for the public to read and soon people were writing in with queries and suggestions of their own. The book contains most of the poems that have been displayed for all the underground travellers. The book is full of different poets, both and new and the poems represent some great subjects like war, love, death, natural world as well as comic verse and nonsense poems. It's a great book and I love it.

MATT DUGGAN

A Journey Across The Pond

Matt Duggan is a poet whose work I will quite happily say
continues to excite and often stun me. I'm proud to say
that Hedgehog will be publishing his collection
Woodworm next year.

When he offered to write an article for us about his
recent visit to the U.S to both read his work and launch another
collection, I didn't take long to accept. Here is what he had to say.
Matt Duggan,
I was heading to the U.S.A with my partner Kelly for a series of poetry
readings that I'd been invited to attend, we travelled on the national
express from Bristol to London to catch the early flight to Boston. How
did all of this come about? Well, the previous year I was very kindly
invited to read for the first time in Boston for the Into the Void Poetry
Competition and what I did notice when attending this event was how
well organised and professional the organisers were, they had vendors
at the event which I've never come across before where the vendors
would take the books from the poets and sell them at the event, giving
the poet the money from any books they sold, it was something very
different to the events that I've attended in the past in the U.K. After
that event I met some quite wonderful and supportive people from a 90
year old Bostonian woman who told me the story of when she served
Dylan Thomas a coffee, (Not just coffee in that cup) what a sweet lady
and such a great lover of poetry I was introduced to her by Daniel
Wuenschel who asked if I would like to come back to Boston again
and do a reading for his prestigious poetry series at Cambridge Public
Library. Well, the answer was a definite yes, but I didn't just want to do
one reading as it wouldn't be worth the trip. Fast forward to a few

months later when I got pleasantly surprised when I was then invited to read in New York at George Wallace's poetry events on the East Side, which would then followed by another invitation to read the following night on Long Island for Peter V Dugan event at Sip This, so my journey across the pond was coming together quite nicely.

I do get very nervous when I read and really didn't know what to expect from these readings across the east-coast, I always felt that as a poet you need to push yourself out of any comfort zones, I needed to push myself and push myself I certainly did. During the time between the first Boston reading in 2017 I had two new chapbooks published 'One Million Tiny Cuts' (Clare Song Birds Publishing House) and 'A Season in Another World' (Thirty West Publishing House). It was Josh the editor at Thirty West Publishing House who suggested that I attend the book launch in Philly after my New York readings which I thought was doable, and something I'd always wanted to do is read at my own book launch in the U.S. and so my journey into the unknown began.

We arrived in Boston and checked into the Buckminster Hotel and by surprise the publishers at Thirty West had sent a nice package of new books for me, which was great, as I only had a few copies left of One Million Tiny Cuts. The hotel which was once where Billie Holiday and Duke Ellington played overlooked the famous Citgo sign and around the corner from the hotel you could see Fenway Park famous for the Red Soxs, not that I know anything about baseball, but you can't help but look at the stadium and go WOW, now that's a big fucking stadium.

The first reading in Boston was held at the Cambridge Public Library with two other guest poets Natalie Shapero and Donald Vincent (Mr Hip) the venue was very close to Harvard so we spent the day travelling around Boston eating doughnuts and watching a re-enactment of the Boston Tea Party and then stopped off to visit the infamous Grolier Bookshop. Daniel the host of the reading had printed off fifty broadsheets of a poem from each of the poets which was handed out to members of the audience. The library itself was on five levels with lots of promo posters and neon signs directing us to a very large auditorium, the audience were a mixture of ages. Daniel gave a wonderful introduction to all of the poets and it was such a great feeling and experience to be reading once again in Boston.

I enjoyed the other two readers of which were both very different in style and content and I found some of Natalie poems were well delivered with more of a prose driven narrative, but I thought obviously aimed at a Boston crowd. Mr Hip poems were more humour driven and hip hop based, but very light hearted and enjoyable. After the event the audience and poets all came together to discuss each performance and you didn't get that cliquey little group heading off into the corner like an amateur boxer in the ring, which I've witnessed many times at poetry events back home. The appreciation I received afterwards was simply awe inspiring and we all headed off for food and drinks in a local bar with discussions on the differences between the poetry scenes in the U.K and the U.S. I got paid more than any reading I've ever done in the U.K. which really helped me out as it's not that I'm money orientated, but it did help, especially with all the travelling that lay ahead of us, plus, a copy of my first collection Dystopia 38.10 (erbacce-press) can now be found in Cambridge Public Library in Boston, which I think is pretty cool.

We travelled the following day on the greyhound from Boston to New York and walked from the bus station through Times Square and found our hotel which was on the 67th floor, the journey in the elevator seemed just as long as the bus journey to Bristol, we then settled in, and headed out into the New York night. My reading was the following afternoon so it gave us time to do a little sightseeing taking in Central Park, Statue of Liberty, and a visit to the Chelsea Hotel. The following day we had lunch and walked through Greenwich Village which was a treat, though some of it had been gentrified. The venue was in a bar called The Parkside Lounge which was on East Houston Street. We sat at the bar after arriving early and met up with George Wallace and what a top guy, we walked through to the seating area at the back of the bar and then met the other guest poet for the event a guy called Jerry Johnson who asked us where in the U.K we were from? It was quite unbelievable that his brother lived a couple of miles from where we live in Bristol. All the readers were of a high standard and I did enjoy the mix of styles and delivery, from a musical accomplishment to moving images used via media downloads, it was an eye opener, and I thoroughly enjoyed reading and felt quite relaxed and not too nervous. The feedback and book sales after were amazing, and I met some lovely poets that I'll never forget, it was also really nice that George came over and complimented me on my set, which was most kind of him.

I felt that I was in a unknown world but I felt very much at home they all made me feel so welcome, it was very much different to previous events that I felt quite embarrassed for some of the events that I'd attended back home, and it was much of the same the following night on Long Island at Peter Dugan event where I read to quite a large crowd in a diner called Sip This, another wonderful well organised evening and to meet Peter and the other Long Island poets was awesome. Would I do it all again, absolutely! But my next stop was Philly for the book launch of my new chapbook 'A Season in Another World'.

We booked in to our hotel and sampled the local cheese steaks before heading to the venue for the book launch and met up with Josh the editor of Thirty West, what a nice chap so down to earth and so full of new and bright ventures he wants to implement for his press who have been so supportive from the edits of the M/S to the cover to the book launch, I really couldn't have asked for more support from a publisher. The venue was about a twenty-minute walk and held at Vox Populi Gallery, which was an old relic of a building and full of some quite interesting urban art installations. The room we had for the book launch was huge and the acoustics were amazing, it was an interesting and perfect venue.

The crowd started to fill up and take their seats as the four guest poets started to read who were mainly Philly based poets apart from Christian Sammartino , it was most interesting to hear them, the differences between the poets in Boston, New York, and Philly. I read quite a long set which was followed by a very inquisitive Q and A from the audience, we then all headed to a local bar where outside while smoking a cigarette with Josh, a rather large looking man approached me, firstly I thought to myself this could be trouble but then he just shook my hand and said "Man, that was a fucking awesome reading, can I buy a book off you" Josh then looked up at me and said "I don't know him, he just arrived at the venue"

It had all come to an end, my readings across the east coast of the U.S. I felt that it was more than worth it, I'd pushed myself away from any comfort zones in Bristol and felt that I had achieved what I wanted. We then strolled through China Town after and then stopped off for food and drunkenly tried to eat Chinese with chop sticks before heading back to JFK for our flight to the U,K.

ANNIE MACLEAN

What Am I Reading?

'I think, therefore I am'
J.O. Morgan: the value of thinking; the excitement of his
poetry. I recommend the poet, J.O. Morgan, and I
recommend every book of his which is in print:

Natural Mechanical	(2009)	CB editions
Long Cuts	(2011)	CB editions
At Maldon	(2013)	CB editions
In Casting Off	(2015)	Happenstance Press
Interference Pattern	(2016)	Jonathan Cape
Assurances	(2018)	Jonathan Cape.

Morgan's publications to date are single book-length poems. His first
book won the Aldeburgh Poetry Prize in 2009. His latest book has
been short-listed for the 2018 Forward Prize. In a Forward Arts
Foundation interview (available online), Morgan discusses his approach
to the composition for each book:
'It takes a lot of thinking to find that right approach ... pushing further
till I hit upon something ... that might just be something special. ...
there's no writing involved, just thinking.'
The interview ends with his advice to a writer:
'Do whatever you feel is necessary, whatever you feel is best, but avoid
the easy options.'

MARTIN MALONE

Mr. Willett's Summertime

It has always struck me as odd that we only really remember or think about the dead and injured of the World Wars and later conflicts, once a year as some sort of set piece morning at the Cenotaph, trying to see how old the Queen looks this year, marvelling at the Chelsea Pensioners who oddly seem to be getting younger every year.

In fact when I started this wee magazine, I was adamant that I wouldn't do a 'War' issue in November, it was why Penny Rimbaud's interview about Wilfred Owen ran in the first magazine and why the cover doesn't feature a poppy this time around.

Saying that, I fear I might be wrong, in fact our sister magazine 'Stickleback' will be launching an issue at 11.11am on the 11th of November, and because perhaps I realised at last that remembering once is better than remembering never. Despite my misgivings about it being impossible to find anything new to say, it shouldn't matter. Not everything has to be shiny and new, some things are too important for that.

All of which formed a backdrop to my first reading of Martin Malone's *Mr. Willett's Summertime*, a beautifully produced pamphlet from Poetry Salzburg, that does what I couldn't imagine and finds a new way to address a subject that, if I can't say has been done-to-death, has certainly been widely explored.

The collection itself is an imagining by Martin that aims to re-create the experience of war from start to end that in its addiction to the details of everyday life becomes more real than a thousand photographs or memoirs have ever managed to make it for me. It avoids, as he suggests, the officer class revisionism of what the war was like as easily as it casts the doubt he sees in Owen's mind, and you almost feel the waves of a sea of ghosts as you read through the collection, but not in the abstract, that would be too easy, instead each ghost has a face and a heart and a life that should have been lived. Which of course is the point. The clever use of new facts (or more rightly, facts that were new to me) such as the Russian, 1st Women's Battalion of Death widens the scope beautifully from what we think we know it must-have-been-like and rightly makes us wonder if we ever knew anything at all.

Martin has a genius for this type of poetry, it is clever in all the right ways and avoids the temptation to preach by creating a very human and humane world for us all to peer into, allowing you to draw conclusions that should have been obvious and leaves you thanking your lucky stars that it was them and not you.

I took the opportunity to ask Martin a few questions about his collection.

I genuinely loved Mr. Willett's Summertime. *I suppose the obvious question is why you decided to write about WW1 (felt able to, maybe) when it was done so well by people who were there?*

"I'm very glad you enjoyed it, Mark. And the parenthesised part of your inquiry really gets to the heart of matters, since it was the very question I asked myself at the start of the project. There is so much hinterland to the Great War as a subject for poetry and, yes, what right had I to believe I could add anything new to the topic when there were writers infinitely more qualified to write about it, by virtue of having been there. One's position – as a non-combatant poet, writing a century after the fact – is ethically questionable at best. That said, there has grown around the subject something of a secondary canon, what the Irish critic Fran Brearton, calls 'post-war Great War poems'. I've written about the subject myself in a chapter from a forthcoming Palgrave-Macmillan Handbook: how the time around the 50th anniversary of the war begat significant sequences of work, by poets such as Ted Hughes, Philip Larkin, Vernon Scannell and Geoffrey Hill. Poetry which was absorbed into our sense of a Great War canon and became as influential upon subsequent writers as the soldier poets themselves. At the outset I sniffed around the topic for quite some time, reading all I could, before deciding that my most ethical route was to write as much about today's world as the world of 1914-1918, though simultaneously, with the Great War acting as a lens through which we see the present. It's not so difficult really, since, as Jon Silkin pointed out when writing about the Great War generation, 'their preoccupations are also ours'. And, if you look at contemporary global politics, you can see disturbing parallels and failures to learn from history. The centenary merely provides chronological symmetry. In this country above all others, I think, the Great War has huge cultural and historical significance. Once I'd decided to use this to my own contemporising ends it was a question of research and hitting upon a poetics adequate to the task.

The more straightforward answer to your question is that I was 'gifted' the Great War as the subject of my PhD. So, it chose me, rather than the other way around. I'd originally wanted to write about the influence of Punk and Post-punk on contemporary poetry but didn't get the funding for that. Probably thanks to the centenary, I did get the funding for this. And having done so, I felt a huge sense of responsibility to represent, with some integrity, a generation whom, I suspect, was better than our own.

Sorry if this is a long answer but it's a subject that's complicated on many levels."

Do you think so far on that perhaps we have lost the soft-focus WW1 had – are people more able to understand the horrors now?

"We have and we haven't. WW1 – as an historical moment – is just so biddable. It gets co-opted by all sorts of people, politics and outlooks. In our lifetime it has certainly tended to have no soft-focus. This has been reflected at most levels of historical study and culture and is almost certainly a product of the surviving poetry above much else. However, while we are in a better position to understand the horrors, time also let's back in some of the factors that brought about the conflict: self-interested elites, misguided patriotism, mistrust of the outsider, egotistical and authoritarian leaders, nationalism and the fragmentation of international unity, to name but a few of the many and complicated reasons for the war. Look at that list. It ought to sound uncomfortably familiar to the citizen of 2014-2018. And there is little doubt that when I started the collection in 2014, there was an appreciable drift towards a sort of neo-con revisionism which was softening the focus once more. Even in popular acts of remembrance I'm attuned to a troublingly aestheticized and top-down mode of commemoration. It still has the lone bugle and sad shires to the fore and is awash with the usual poppy show. This has always troubled me. Hence poems like 'Dear Revisionist', and an attempt to widen scrutiny in order to remind us Great War-obsessed Brits that this was a global tragedy endured by both sides, which made victims of everyone. To be lectured at, once more, by public-school elites and the usual officer class stuck in my craw. Then again, look around and you see the least socially mobile society in the developed world, so while there may never be 'such innocence again' there is certainly a relapse towards such deference; a subject I deal with in a poem like 'Downturn', which punningly refers to our kinky, kiss-ass love of the old upstairs-downstairs world of the Edwardian costume drama. It's one of the reasons that, in The Unreturning sequence certainly, I'm dressing up WW1 in twenty-first century garb whenever possible."

I was interested to hear how you approached the collection. Did it entail a lot of research as a one-off, or is it a topic you had a long-term interest in?

"I think I may have already answered this in passing. It entailed a lot of research funded as a one-off project in the form of my PhD, but that in turn has nurtured a long-term interest. In terms of approaching the collection per se, it was mainly a question of scoping out a poetics adequate to the task of doing the subject justice and squaring my own ethical dilemma of writing about the Great War in the first place. Jacob Polley recently said something like: "one of the main tasks of writing involves the search for technique". And I now know what he means. This is the first collection I've written where I was aware of the need to consciously develop a unifying approach to the verse. I've written about it at length, in an essay published in the Book 2.0 journal, called 'Prized assets of a ghost economy' but it was evolving all the time. Doing a practice-led critical study of the Great War for my PhD was a new and productive way of working, I think. Though, whether I shall ever again get three years paid time in which to write a poetry collection, I very much doubt. I suppose my approach is clearest in the prose poem title sequence, a pair of which you published in Issue #2. In some ways, what you've encountered in Mr. Willett's Summertime was me writing in that lyric-elegiac mode most readily associated with Great War verse. But that was done in order to let me deviate from the mode in the answering prose poem sequence of The Unreturning, which is both a self-conscious refusal to behave like Great War lyrics and intended to look physically like rows of gravestones in a war cemetery. These 10-line, block-justified poems deliberately wear their conceits to the fore, as 21st-century reconstructions of a century old conflict written by someone who is clearly here and not 'there'. The touchstones being someone like Geoffrey Hill and certain features of early modernism."

Are there new stories to be found, or lessons to be learned?
"There certainly are and I hope that *Mr. Willett's Summertime* has proved it to a degree. You see, once you start researching a conflict as vast as the Great War, you are bound to uncover hundreds of stories and perspectives that deviate from the easily digestible core narratives we are fed year in year out. Coupled with the multi-directional memory approach of The Unreturning, I can honestly say that it would be possible for me to write about or, rather, through the Great War for the rest of my life, should I choose. Thankfully, Armistice arrived for me once I'd finished the manuscript, though there may be a clean-up operation yet to be gone through with my editor. Poems like 'The Turnip Winter', 'An-sky's Lament' and 'The 1st Women's Battalion of Death' ought to flag up the sheer variety of hitherto under-scrutinised perspectives and narratives surrounding WW1. And it's not just the war itself that is awash with possibilities, the whole social and cultural response to it is material also. Indeed, while I studied the poets of WW1, my spirit guides were just as much the war artists also; a fact evident in the number of poems about painters like Nevinson, Nash and Gilman. As for the new lessons to be learned, I hope the reader

will soon become aware of the book's contemporising drift and aspiration."

How long did the collection take to come together?

"Well, I handed the PhD in bang on time, so three years. But one or two of the poems were written before this collection as a result of my interest in the artists mentioned above and I was adding to it up until I handed it over to my prospective publisher."

How did you come to have the collection published by Poetry Salzburg, and did going with an Austrian publisher 'mean' anything?

"Well, I've Keith Hutson to thank for that. He joined their editorial team and asked me to submit something. I sent them *Mr. Willett's Summertime* and thankfully they went for it. Poetry Salzburg are a quality imprint so I was very glad to go with them. I love the hint of Russian Constructivism in their corporate covers and Wolfgang Görtschacher is a nice guy and a knowledgeable editor. The fact that they're Austrian is a co-incidental bonus, given the internationalist perspective I wanted to throw upon the war. Also, some of the early poems came out of a research trip to Vienna I did in the Summer of 2014. I've good friends there and knew that the Austro-Hungarian perspective on the Great War might be an interesting place to start. Many years ago, I witnessed the funeral cortege of the last Austro-Hungarian princess, Zeta. So, the 'meaning' is as much personal as it is symbolic..."

There is a very personal feeling to the poetry – not so much reportage a lot of the time, but you really seem to get inside people's heads. For instance, can you tell us about 'Let Us Sleep Now'.

"...which leads nicely into this question! 'Let Us Sleep Now' came from that very trip to Vienna mentioned above. It was exactly 100 years to the day that the war was starting as I sat on the station platform described in the poem. A hot sunny afternoon when I was people watching and saw a young Austrian guy heading up the line towards Simmering on the tram. I just channelled a bit of the compassion of Owen's 'Strange Meeting' and wrote an update (the title is, actually, the final phrase of that poem). When I got back to Wiener Neustadt, my friends told me that Simmering is the location of one of Vienna's big cemeteries. So, fate had gifted me all kinds of resonance that afternoon. I suppose, a form of empathetic penetration into people's heads and lives is just something poets are supposed to do. As the opening poem 'Séance' suggests, one has to listen to voices conjured from the past and represent them to the contemporary reader. Poetry isn't reportage really, is it? I'm just about to teach an online module on voice for Aberdeen University, so hopefully, the experience of writing this book will stand me in good stead. And I'm giving a paper on his poetic afterlife to the Wilfred Owen Conference at Oxford in October. All grist to the mill, hopefully."

Can you talk us through your thinking for 'The 1st Women's Battalion of Death' and 'Sorley's Bullet'?

"Those two poems come from very different circumstances, the first purely from research, the second from personal coincidence similar to 'Let Us Sleep Now'. 'The 1st Women's Battalion of Death' was one of those many narratives to be uncovered during my research, the sort lost to a national story tending towards the subaltern poetry of the Western Front, as it is in the U.K. Apart from being a wonderful gift of a title, the story of Bochkareva and the Russian women's battalions put into the field on the Eastern Front resonated with today's struggle for equality and the recent frontline deployment of women in the U.K.'s armed forces. It's nothing new and surely a bittersweet development. 'Sorley's Bullet' was actually a poem commissioned by Aberdeen University for their Mayfest 2015, to celebrate the centenary of Sorley's death at the Battle of Loos in October, 1915. However, there were numerous personal touch-points too. I'd just moved up here and found out that one of my favourite Great War poets had been born just up the road in Don Street. And I shared with Sorley a great love of the Kennet Valley. He'd gone to school at Marlborough and used to wander and run the downland surrounding it, as I myself had done when I lived in the villages of West Overton and Avebury. Also, just as he'd written about that landscape in his posthumous collection, Marlborough and Other Poems, I'd written a fair bit about it in The Waiting Hillside. It seemed fated, then. The title, 'Sorley's Bullet' is an allusion to a line from one of his famous war poems, 'All the hills and vales along...'. I'm also writing a chapter on his wonderful Letters for a book that I'm co-editing on Scottish Great War writing. A virtuous, though tragic, circle then."

More generally, you are leaving The Interpreter's House behind now, why is that?

"I'm leaving it simply because, when I took it over in 2013, I said that I'd do it for 5 years and 15 issues. I'm a man of my word. Temperamentally, I'd have gone for three years but that felt too short and five was sufficient unto the day."

What are you planning to do next?

"Hm. Quite a few people have been asking me that of late. To be honest, I am simply knackered and feeling a bit burnt out. It's been a hard five years. I'd like to try writing some short stories and concentrate a little more on my own poetry, but, out of necessity, I am now back in full-time employment. Despite a PhD and three MAs, I can't seem to even get an interview for academic jobs. So, while I try to create my own, with the development of online courses for Aberdeen, I'm back to full-time school-teaching, having committed a form of 'pension suicide' in order to do the PhD. Also, I've an absolutely gorgeous but full-on 4-year old who takes up a lot of time and a new/old house up on the Moray coast. Little wonder I'm a bit distracted right now. That said, I've made the switch to a new font, which I always do when I start a new collection. I've now gone from Times New Roman to Calibri to Georgia to the current Garamond. So, I've stated my intent, at least, by opening up a new font in the great war against silence. Sorry, it becomes a habit of mind."

Mr Willett's Summertime by Martin Malone is available from www.poetrysalzburg.com

HANNAH BROCKBANK

Bloodlines

So much great poetry, like any art, can come from pain and in *Bloodlines* it would be easy to suggest that Hannah Brockbank's poetry, influenced as it is by a missing parent - her father - is a simple response to a childhood loss. In the hands of many poets, perhaps that would be the case, but then Hannah isn't just any poet and *Bloodlines* is far from just yet-another-pamphlet.

Taking a loss and extrapolating it into a wider context, Hannah has - like Martin Malone with *Mr Willett's Summertime* - created an imagined world of feelings and events that quite easily *could* have been, and then played with it to make a wider point. It did in fact strike me just what a brilliant approach she has taken here and how assured her handling of what, let's face it, could have felt overwhelming in both the personal and the emotive. In truth, Hannah writes with a cold-eyed certainty that seems to allow her a third-eyed-perspective taking her beyond both a simplistic emotional response and contrived metaphor as easily as it tears tears from your eyes.

The only downside to all of this is that I'm not quite sure Hannah realises just what an epic collection she has created here and for her, if not us, there is always the problem of following it up.

As ever, I was pleased to take the chance to talk to Hannah about this.

I'm not sure that I have ever read a collection that distils so many emotions into such a short space. How did it feel once you had finished the poems?
"I wasn't looking for a sense of catharsis when I wrote *Bloodlines,* but it was pleasing to organise my experience into a narrative arc. I chose the

115

experience of growing up without a father because it has been an interesting and complex situation for me. I've always been more curious than upset about my absent father. I can also see that there is the potential for retraumatising oneself, and it should be a serious consideration before anyone starts such an intensely personal project. All things considered, I was thankful and relieved at what I'd managed to achieve. Most importantly, the creation of *Bloodlines*, made me acutely aware that poetry is the most apposite mode of expression for me, and the satisfaction I gained from communicating my experience and emotion, consolidated my love of writing poetry."

I got the sense, reading it, that they are very much a set of poems that came as one. I don't know if that is true or not, so can you talk a little about how you came to write the collection and what drove you?

"*Bloodlines* was created over ten months and formed part of my MA in Creative Writing at the University of Chichester. I'd contemplated writing about my experience of growing up without a father for some time and considered myself emotionally prepared to tackle it but writing about it didn't become a truly conscious decision until I became a parent. Issues surrounding biological inheritance, particularly during pregnancy health checks, highlighted the fact that there were so many unanswered questions, and when my daughter was finally born, the simultaneous feeling of complete love and utter fear, reinforced the staggering responsibility of parenthood. I could, for the first time, acknowledge the gravity of my biological father's decision to be absent. It is worth noting though, that acknowledging is vastly different from understanding, and I will always be unendingly curious about human nature."

The aspect of your writing that continually blows me away is that there is this very personal and considered humanity to it. Every word and line clearly matter, but you have still managed to present it as a piece of work. How easy did you find it to detach yourself when it came to building, editing and everything else that goes into it becoming a book?

"I don't detach myself to begin with. Most of my poems begin with an image, but in this instance, there were few images amassed from lived experience. I have one photograph of my father and mother together on an outing to the coast, and a couple of formal wedding photographs. As a result, most of the poems in Bloodlines evolved from deep-seated emotions. The first step was to acknowledge those emotions, sit with them, and feel comfortable enough to write them down.

I wrote copious amounts at first, deliberately not making any edits. Only when I'd exhausted that initial stage, did I start to shape the poems, for example, paying attention to line ends and internal rhyme, and making sure that every word hauled its weight. I was more detached during this process, as I wanted the poems to communicate effectively and be polished. One of the best ways to do this, is to put them through the rigour of a trusted workshop group."

I get the sense that you know exactly what you are doing - are you confident in your work in that you know what each poem should be, how it will be presented?

"At first, I'm never completely confident that a poem will succeed, but experimenting with words and redrafting is one of the most enjoyable components of writing for me. I think confidence begins to build as the poem develops, becomes stronger and more refined. By the third or fourth draft, I'm more confident about what it's communicating and that it contains all the elements to support that. If I am not completely happy with a poem, I'll let it marinade for a bit before working on it again, and I certainly won't submit the poem anywhere until I am satisfied of its quality.

Studying for an MA in Creative Writing reinforced my knowledge and writing skills. Attending externally led workshops was also extremely helpful. You can learn a lot from readings and talking to other poets about their writing experiences."

I love your use of folklore - is that something you draw on a lot in your work?

"No, not really. I'm more drawn to realism and in particular love writing poems set in domestic situations or on the South Downs. I enjoy etymology and discovering words rooted in nature and landscape as they can make writing less abstract and more entrenched in locality and identity, which is far more powerful, in my opinion."

Can I ask you to give a brief description of two or three of the poems in the book?

Myling
"Mylings feature in Scandinavian Folk-belief. They are the spirits of unbaptised children abandoned in the wilderness by their relations. Mylings and their story of abandonment are of great interest to me for obvious reasons. I wanted to make the Myling children visible again and one way of doing that was through poetry."

Sand
"'Sand' was an exploration of another facet of biological inheritance; physical appearance and the relation between parts. The inspiration came after a visit to The Barbara Hepworth Museum and Sculpture Garden, where I particularly enjoyed viewing the sculpture, Spring, 1965. I loved the way the lines drew me inside the ovoid and trained my eyes on the inner surfaces. Where the lines start, intersect and end all carried meaning. I could see parallels not only with the use of line in poetry, but also the lines of my physical form. Where did my long spine come from, or my earlobes that attach?"

Being nosey, I noticed that you had completed a residency at the Museum of Motherhood. Can you tell us about that and the work that has come out of it?
"I am currently studying for a Ph.D. at the University of Chichester. The Ph.D. consists of two components, the first being the creation of a new full-length collection of poems based on my experience of mothering, and the second component is an accompanying study on matrifocal poetry.

As part of my Ph.D., I applied for a two-week residency at the Museum of Motherhood (M.O.M.) in Florida, USA, and was successful in my application. During my residency I was able to respond creatively to the wealth of exhibits and art at M.O.M., which incorporated a range of mothering concepts and further inspired me to embody my own mothering experience through poetry. The new poems are concerned with my physical and psychological transformation within the praxis of mothering."

Who was the first poet/the first poems you read that made you think that you would like to write?

"Vicki Feaver's *The Book of Blood* (Jonathan Cape, 2006) was the first collection that truly resonated with me. Feaver's awesome, ferocious imagery and the strength of her voice gave me confidence, and I clearly remember feeling liberated after reading it. Her poetry gave me permission to write about my own experiences of the quotidian and the domestic."

What are you planning next?

"I am going to finish my Ph.D. first. Then I will begin to research and write my second collection of poetry. I keep a notebook for future projects and ideas going all the time. I'm also looking forward to finishing an illustration project for a children's book."

Bloodlines by Hannah Brockbank is available from www.indigodreams.co.uk

ZACK DICKS

The Gloucester Poetry Festival

Poetry and indeed writer festivals have taken over the literary landscape over the last few years, but few have managed to create an understated and generally chilled vibe in the way that the Gloucester Poetry Festival has. So what is involved in creating a festival and doesn't it kill your own art? I caught up with the man behind Gloucester, Zack Dicks to find out.

How did the Gloucester Festival come about and what was your involvement?
"The festival came about from my idea that Gloucester needed a poetry festival. In 2016 I started linking poets, performers, designers, venues and created a core team of people to develop a poetry scene in Gloucester. My involvement with this was the planning and execution. We wanted to create an ethos around poetry so inexperienced poets could perform with established folks and pull all the writers out of the woodwork. Last year, Derek Dohren performed for the first time at the festival and has gone on to headline all over the country. He has stated that a big part of this is down to the encouragement and support he has received by the Gloucester Poetry Society (I organise both). Gloucester has always had a rebellious past and we wanted that reflected in how we do things a bit differently. We wanted to have poetry parties not just readings."

Can you tell us a little about your background as a poet - I know you have a collection coming out soon, what inspired that?

"I've always been a writer, at school, I had the word 'potential' dangled over me like a sword, 'dark horse' was another phrase. Teachers thought I was lazy, this year whilst doing my masters in Creative and Critical Writing it was established that I was dyslexic; despite going to a grammar school this was never identified until now and in hindsight has altered my outlook on life and writing.

One teacher at school, who shall remain nameless, stated I was 'nothing but a malcontent'. This stuck with me. I wrote as this malcontent throughout my twenties without really realising there were others like me writing. I never knew poetry was alive. I thought it died with Hughes. Nobody I knew wrote and because of that I scribbled in secret.

My collection is called *Malcontent* as a result of these experiences and are an eclectic mix of poems looking at the world through the eyes of this rebel figure, dissatisfied with politics and day to day life."

Thinking about the festival - who was the first poet you booked that made you sit back and think it could become something special?

"That's tough, the problem I have is that the poets I really admire are all my friends, I met them through poetry events and invited them to perform, so it's a tough one to answer. The performers that stood out though, as having a certain buzz, were Chloë Jacquet at our first event, there was so much excitement to see her perform and a huge round of applause, Nick Lovell too and Clive Oseman too. They have such a presence. All three are multi slam winners and quality page poets to boot."

There are a lot of festivals these days, people seem to love the experience now more than ever of sharing poetry aloud, what makes Gloucester different from some of the others?

"We break the mould, quote a cliché. We have a massive number of guest poets at our events up to eight and they are all top-notch poets. I was told having longer events wouldn't work but it's been proven it does. I remember last year, one event (Feline Fonics) we had all our guest poets and the open mic was complete. We were just winding

down and there was a call for more, we ended up going on for quite
some time, this happened several times at the festival. I love this
because it takes on a life of its own, with all the wonder that goes with
it."

*I hate to think how much time organising a festival takes - does it take
over your life?*

"Yes and no, the first year yes, as it was all new and connections had to
be made but now the team is growing, so we have marketing,
development and events organising planned way in advance. It takes
time to set up each of the events but after it's the slow drops that fill the
tank. I did worry I wouldn't have time to write but in actual fact I end
up writing more to perform at the festival. It would be rude not to read
some of your own stuff and it encourages others to be involved too."

*Do you feel it has an impact upon your own writing and is this positive
or negative?*

"It could be negative if I got bogged down and didn't plan effectively
but as we get the venues arranged early on and book poets as we go it's
not too much of an impact. I always give myself a few minutes to do
bursts of writing in a day and come back to it sporadically. I like to
graze at a poem until I'm full so I always have time to write."

*It surprises me that there is still a performance Vs. page mentality in
poetry, but Gloucester seems to manage the crossover well. Was that
something you were conscious of having to negotiate?*

"Massively. I've always considered myself a page poet who dabbles in
performance. I think it comes from your deixis. To many, I'm a
performance poet and others a page poet. It comes down to bias.
There are different rules for both and I've noted the conflict comes
from both mediums trying to excel, as they should. An example would
be a page poet being concise and trimming a poem like a bonsai tree,
where every word is working. A performance poet wouldn't use that
strategy as they want as many people to observe a plant and would want
a big huge growth that is as large as a building, every branch wild, to be
seen as it always under the pressure of the wind. The wind being the
outside influence of the audience. Performance poets want their work
to interact on an immediate level and page poems can need a little time

to digest. It doesn't surprise me about conflict as people who think they are right and disagree will argue. The trick is knowing there is a middle ground where you can do both. I would advise anyone performing a poem when you are not sure about the audience leanings, to specify the type of poem intended, page or performance, as it can influence the way it is perceived. In Gloucester we believe there is a place for all poetry and examine a poem based on what a poet wants to do with it before critically analysing it. A push bike makes a lousy boat."

More generally, do you feel that songwriting and Rap can be considered poetry?

"Many forms of poetry could be sung and RAP is by definition 'Rhythm and Poetry'. Going back to points on page vs. performance, in my opinion a song doesn't speak to me, on paper, as well as it's sung and neither does Rap because they are supposed to be delivered orally.

Similarly, a lot of poets seem to walk a fine line between poetry and stand-up, would you ever not book somebody because they were too funny?

"No, I don't see there being an issue with humour as long as it's done well. I've seen some where there is say 90% comedy and 10% poetry content and that is less appealing as the comedy should derive from the poetry and not the comedy set. If we were focussed on comedy first it wouldn't be an issue but we are after funny poetry."

Who are you looking forward to most at this year's festival?

"Wow, that's tough Skot Cowley aka the Rusty Goat has recently branched into poetry and I'm looking forward to his observations. We have Rick Sanders who is incredibly witty and Angie Belcher too, these will be some of the highlights for me."

Tell us why we should all come along?

"It's judgement free, if you like chilled page poetry, we have that, or if you prefer edgy performers, we can do that too. We have some exceptional talent that comes to Gloucester and anyone can get up and perform alongside them. I feel that is incredibly empowering. We are in the poetry business and we nurture talent. Poetry is for everyone and it's our party." Find out more at:
www.facebook.com/GloucesterPoetryFestival

Z.D. DICKS

The Peacock

At a farm-park a toddler with a duckling blonde tuft
pinballs between shed cages
He stares up at beaks and feather eyebrows
bald heads and dirty fluff collars
red suited mimics and masked aces
All shivering in winter wind

The boy trundles in un-scuffed boots and elasticated combats
arms raised
a flightless bird loose in the courtyard
through pot-hole puddles kicking straw
past a swinging half-open dutch door
around a corner to a picnic bench
alongside a bush-bulged wire-mesh fence

Little feet stop and a pudgy back bends
a pendulum face swings low under a bird neck
scanning shades of metallic blue
soft fingers creep out
he tip-toes forward and plump lips coo

A trumpet sounds and a fan ruffles
a baby falls back on a light thick nappy
green and blue feather eyes splay in a crescent
                              mock predators eyes above
A fog horn bellows from pincers of bone
closing blades connect
                    peck
                          and shove

Crawling on palms and patellas
a baby boy bounces up
runs like a cowboy after a long ride
beaten slashed and bruised

I want a peacock

It's my favourite

For the next 6 months a horn woke the neighbours
we had brought a peacock home to stay
An ill flying bird who sang on command
in a phase we knew wouldn't last
                              of pecking us each day

I lik chees
Chies is good
Chedder is grate
But Gouda
Is gooder

IT'S GOOD. YOU
JUST NEED TO CHANGE
ALL THE WORDS.

postcards from the hedge
@mooseallain